Living
Synergistically

By Thomas D. Willhite

PUBLISHED BY
PSI PUBLISHING
9TH PRINTING
ISBN 0-9659994-2-4
ALL MATERIALS ©2000 PSI SEMINARS, L.L.C.

psi seminars
strategies for life success

LIBRARY OF CONGRESS CATALOGING-IN-PUBLICATION DATA

WILLHITE, THOMAS D., 1940-1983
LIVING SYNERGISTICALLY / THOMAS WILLHITE
P.   CM.
ISBN 0-9659994-2-4
1. SELF-IMPROVEMENT 2. PSYCHOLOGY

PRINTED IN THE UNITED STATES OF AMERICA

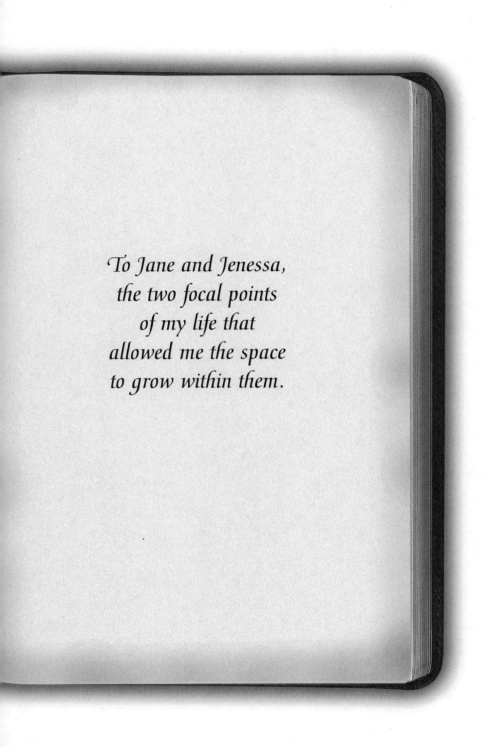

To Jane and Jenessa,
the two focal points
of my life that
allowed me the space
to grow within them.

CONTENTS

PREFACE

*"Part of the price you must pay
for any knowledge is to discover
it for yourself."*

Nothing in this world is new...not this book...nor the paper on which it is printed. The very atoms which comprise my body and yours are ancient. Though their arrangement - the way they are combined - is new, the atoms themselves are old.

Similarly, there are no new truths. The Truth is and always has been and always will be. I can neither add to nor take away from the Truth. All I can do is present it as I understand it and as I see it applying to the NOW.

All truths are universal. I cannot teach them; no one can. You already have access to them. Instead, the function of this book and of PSI Seminars is to educate - which means "to draw out" truths.

PSI is not a religion; therefore, it cannot be in conflict with any religious beliefs. PSI is a vehicle, which can be used by each individual to get from where they are to where they want to go...to create peace of mind, liberty, love, and wisdom in their lives.

The understanding of the concepts contained in this book - and applied in the PSI seminars - have dramatically changed thousands upon thousands of lives. If you keep an open mind as you examine these concepts, I believe you can alter the course of your life, too. The concepts, if digested and made a part of your everyday world, will give you "life more abundantly."

The way I recommend you read this book, the way in which you will benefit the most, is to be in touch with yourself. Do not look for confirmations. Rather, scrutinize your feelings with one thought in mind - Truth. Be conscious of your inner reactions, whether positive, negative or perhaps no reaction at all. Be prepared to step aside and ask, "Why am I reacting this way?" or "What is being said that makes me feel this way?" If you do this, I believe you will discover some important things about yourself. Remember... discovery, growth, and change must begin with you.

I suggest that you be alone when you read this book. Inspiration, creativity, and growth come easier when you are in a peaceful atmosphere. Allow enough time to know yourself better. Be relaxed and, most importantly - be gentle with yourself?

Finally, know that there is a price for all things. There is a price for this book...there is a price for every PSI seminar...there is a price for every success. I have never had anything free in my life. Not ever! Nor have you. Wisdom is being able to determine what the price is when it comes.

Part of the price you must pay for any knowledge is to discover it for yourself. You must learn your own lessons...you must make your own mistakes...you must pay your own prices...You must create your own life's story.

Thomas D. Willhite

$\mathcal{F}$OREWORD I

I was first introduced to Tom Willhite in Las Cruces, New Mexico, in July 1972. Although I had gained some ground in my own search for peace of mind, there were many frustrations, resulting from goals unachieved, and many obstacles still standing between myself and those goals. In 1972, I was coming to the end of a term as County Clerk of Doña Ana County, New Mexico. It had been four years of responsibility and growth for me, and I wanted to continue my public service. I was not eligible for re-election as County Clerk, so I was determined to become the first woman elected to the State Senate from my part of the state.

There were many obstacles in the way of such a goal. The incumbent was seeking re-election; there would be primary election opposition from my own party, and old traditions would have to be challenged. If elected. I would be the third woman in the history of the state to be elected to the State Senate.

In April 1972, I filed for the office of Senator. Shortly thereafter, my good friend Conrad Salas, who had already been taught the secrets of this book by Tom Willhite, came to see me. Conrad was himself a candidate for the New Mexico House of Representatives. He shared with me some of the things he had learned from Tom, and with his help I won the June primary.

Conrad was so excited about what was happening to him after graduating form Tom's class (he went on to win his election to the House of Representatives) that two of my sons attended. Finally, I myself enrolled in the Las Cruces class in July of 1972.

During that four-day experience, I learned how to overcome, not only the obstacles to election, but also the obstacles to areas of personal growth I had all but given up on. I and my fellow students learned what it means to "live synergistically." We learned how to apply within every aspect of our lives the great truths and Universal Laws - how to make them work for, and not against, us. Long before election day, I and many other graduates were using these laws and working with the techniques from the seminar to insure my election.

Results on election night were as expected. I had won; I (should say we) had defeated the incumbent senator by a vote of 5131 to 3283. Since my swearing in as New Mexico State Senator form Doña Ana County District 37 on January 2, 1973, I have met many obstacles successfully and have enjoyed even more growth and success than I had ever imagined. Many people say that it was simply luck or fate that put me in the State Senate. But those of us who have begun to confront the person inside of us and to take control of our own lives and destinies know better. We have seen the truth; and as we strive to know and apply the truth, the truth will set us free. As you read the book, ask yourself what could really be yours if you were all you could be... In the following pages you may find some of your own questions being asked. Don't be surprised if the answers don't come easily, if they are not in bold face at the top of each page. They won't be. The price of discovery is the search itself, and only you can pay it. The secrets in this book will be revealed to those who will make the effort. If you want success badly enough, you must weigh each thought, action and experience. The reward you reap will be the knowledge of some of history's best kept secrets, which when understood and applied will truly guide you to the success in life that all have dreamed about, but only a few have attained. I am ...

Gladys Hansen
State Senator
New Mexico

$\mathcal{F}$OREWORD II

Christmas, 1974

A Message from Hawaii...

Tom Willhite's invitation to write these words comes at an unusual time - a time when people seek to tune their senses to the keenest pitch. This is the end of a momentous year for our Spaceship Earth, hopefully a "turning point year" to mark a more certain course toward a greater sense of responsibility - for our lives, for our fellow human beings, and for our finite resources.

A few short hours ago I sat at the edge of Kilauea Crater witnessing one of the fiery volcanic eruptions for which the big island of Hawaii is famous. Here, on what has been described as the most isolated archipelago on Earth, with a full Hawaiian moon above my head, I pondered in awe the stupendous forces which are at work, shaping our world - and our ideas. The bright foundations of lava are the inevitable result of a steady build-up of pressure within the volcano. It is exciting to think that this molten part of our Earth has been gradually shifting toward this one dramatic spectacle for eons and now becomes new land for Hawaii.

People are like this. Ideas are like this. In this volume which you are about to read, you will be directed to think about ideas as things with lives, rhythms, and destinies. You will be confronted with the inexorable growth and decay which our ideas, indeed our selves, must confront - but not helplessly.

Watching the lava fountains reminds me of the significance of this special land, entirely primitive until 1778. Here, perhaps more than anywhere on Earth, we have not just an opportunity, but a responsibility to shift and blend those best elements of East and West: the contemplative, inner-directed, mystical Orient and the bustling. assertive, manipulative Occident.

Time...Ideas...Everything keeps coming back to central truth...

"Living Synergistically" might represent to the Western person those basic ideas of right living which the Chinese have burnished these many centuries to describe the superior person. Tom Willhite has put together thoughts and ideas which are deceptively simple; and were it not for the intriguing word "synergistically," one might pass over the contents superficially saying, "I've heard it before." This is exactly why we can not longer afford this escape. The ideas expressed in this modest volume have the impact, the persistence of a lava flow. Now, in the last quarter of the twentieth century, we are forced to acknowledge that the flow is headed in the direction of our house! Watershed is not an adequate term: ours is a lavish generation. Either we will acknowledge and chart our course by principles of right living - and you will find them beautifully stated here - or the civilization we value will be extinguished. Awesome threat? Yes. Exciting challenge? Yes!

We are so unresponsive to the great spiritual truths. We have been exposed to them to the point that we no longer hear, feel, see them. When Christ appeared to his disciples after the crucifixion, he assured them he would leave a counselor - a comforter - with them. The crisis we are enduring now aboard Spaceship Earth is clear evidence that we fail to recognize or use this marvelous gift - the counselor.

Tom Willhite steers us back in the direction of reuniting ourselves with this spiritual force. A century or more has passed since dynamic psychiatry came upon the scene in the Western world. I believe we have had time to measure and evaluate to some degree the forces which motivate humanity. The unconscious - fiery, compelling, indiscriminating - is not more destructive than it is constructive. Like the volcano, it creates something new. It is raw energy and, in the realm of ideas, it is opportunity. Our Hawaiian Kahuna, the ancient spiritual leader, regarded the unconscious as a little brother with vast resources, energies, intuition and creativity. The unconscious was, by loving attention and counsel, to be made into humanity's partner along the life path. The energy derived from this alliance would carry humanity to its ultimate destiny: spiritual fulfillment.

Read these pages slowly and, as Tom suggests, in solitude. But do more than this. Thoughts by themselves are never enough - the Master never healed anyone without assigning a task. If now, belatedly, you have discovered that your life is borne on a current "too full for sound or foam," then choose to live synergistically. Seek out your Pilot! Chart your course! Get on with it!

John Cummins Mebane, M.D., F.A.P.A.
Diplomat, American Board of Psychiatry and Neurology
Chief, Hawaii Community Mental Health Center

ℒIVING ℒYNERGISTICALLY

"In the ocean of life the isles of blessedness are awaiting and the sunny shore of your ideals awaits your coming."
- James Allen

A life of synergism is one in which each person can attain total peace of mind. It is the answer. It is that certain something that most people strive to achieve even without being aware of it. In the chapters that follow, I will cover the necessary thought processes required for truly "living synergistically."

To begin with, let us realize that synergistic living is developed totally from within. People spend most of their time in the physical world of the intellect - the conscious mind. As a result, they blame outside circumstances or bad luck for their lack of progress. Yet it is only when a person discovers the inner levels of the subconscious and superconscious minds that they will move toward control of their environment.

Living synergistically is conceptual living. It is

a method of existence, a thought pattern or thought process. It is an attitude, a way by which humanity can exist harmoniously and live in peace. In fact, it is the only way humanity can live in peace. By harmonizing all levels of thinking as one, internal peace of mind is created. When a person has total peace of mind, this is, in fact, synergistic living.

Synergistic living begins with the awareness of the various levels of consciousness. There are three levels: the conscious, subconscious, and superconscious minds. To clarify this, let us relate the three levels of consciousness to a three-story house. On the first floor is the conscious mind. The conscious mind is a realm of logic and reasoning, or physical awareness. As a rule, people inhabit but a small percentage of this floor. On the second floor we find a person's subconscious mind - their intuition, inspiration, and creativity. People also spend very little time here. This second level is a necessary transition or middle stage; much of the flow of inspiration and universal power from the third floor, the superconscious, is cut off here. The third floor, the superconscious - source of universal power - is rarely used. For the most part, it is not known to the average person. Most assuredly it is there, waiting to be drawn upon; but lack of awareness keeps this power virtually inactive.

When people become aware that they are the vehicle through which this universal power can flow, then they can accomplish all things. However, until they become aware of these three levels of consciousness and learn how to maintain all three working together, synergism cannot occur.

The conscious mind is incapable of understanding the superconscious mind, and yet the superconscious mind will feed the conscious mind ideas and inspiration through the subconscious mind as long as the channels are open. The following analogy may help to describe how this universal power flows through us.

Picture in your mind a sweltering day. Out in the yard, lying on the grass, is a garden hose, rolled up in an orderly fashion, immobile but prepared for action...ready to be of service. It is a vehicle for the life-giving element of water, but it can give nothing and is of no value until the spigot is cracked open. When opened, the water may first come through as just a trickle. Take a drink from that hose and you will probably find that the hose contains stagnant water and perhaps tastes a little rubbery. The water was clean and pure when it left the spigot, but it has picked up impurities from the garden hose. Now, turn the spigot on full force! Taste the water again... is it not fresh and pure? This water has not had time to stagnate from lack of use.

So it is with people. Become aware that people are much like the garden hose. They are the vehicle through which universal power will flow - when allowed to flow.

Universal power is ever present, but it may be stagnant from inactivity. People have the ability to reach up, crack the valve, and allow this "water" to flow through themselves. The degree to which they open the spigot will regulate the amount and quality of water coming through the hose. It is your choice. You can allow it to flow through yourself abundantly, or you can turn it off and say, "Well, I'm stupid and a slow learner and just can't do those things". We need to discover how to allow this universal power to flow through us, and how to put its life-giving force to use in our lives.

Most men and women live lives of "quiet desperation." I call this type of person, "John Averageman." For the most part John Averageman feels locked into his or her average position, whatever that might be. It's because of this locked up feeling that a person will stop trying to do more, be more, and grow more. We say they appear stable: but basic scientific studies tell us that, at any given time the so-called stable elements of the earth are changing. Either they are gathering substance of free energy, or they are expelling energy. In truth, nothing is really stable at all. All substances are either growing or decaying at any one point in time. Human beings are no exception. If we are not growing, then we are decaying.

We all know members of our society who strive to be unheard and unnoticed. They seek no authority and risk no acceptance of responsibility. In short, they cannot be blamed for what they have not done... all for the sake of remaining normal, average, and stable. However, what they fail to realize is that there is no real stability. Perhaps that is why the stability seekers feel and, consequently, manifest insecurity and inner turmoil. They are in a state of decay because they are not growing.

There are other members of our society who constantly live with inner turmoil. They expect so much of themselves that they find it difficult to live up to those expectations. This type of person will usually have difficulty giving others "space" to make mistakes and, subsequently, grow. These people are frequently the most unfeeling prosecutors when it comes to their own mistakes. They are not growing either.

If we are to begin to grow instead of decay, we do, indeed, have a great deal to learn about this term "synergism." We need to develop an understanding of the basic concepts and laws of the universe and to begin to apply them to our own lives.

Most people want desperately to live by the "do unto others" concept, which is a key to synergism, but they have not really understood the meaning of this law. People swallow many beliefs; but until they have been digested, these beliefs do not become a part of them. When a person uses others to further their own ends or to accomplish their goals, they become an exploiter. Synergism cannot exist when exploitation occurs. Exploitation results in inner turmoil, confusion, frustration, and illness. It opposes synergism.

Selfishness and greed are terms which are often linked to exploitation. We tend to use these terms interchangeably when, in fact, there is a great difference between the two. All individuals have wants and needs. When a person is selfish, they are willing to pay the price for whatever their wants may require. Greed, however, is the uncontrollable furtherance of selfishness. A person shows their greed when they are not willing to pay the price required in order to fulfill their wants and desires. They take from others and thus, become an exploiter.

Humanity needs to understand these basic laws and concepts and digest them...apply them to their lives...rather than to simply acknowledge their existence. By understanding and practicing these laws, such as the "do unto others concept, one can begin to overcome the decay of the "stability syndrome" and can begin a new, synergistic type of growth pattern. If we do so, then we will sway from our program of exploitation toward a path of peaceful co-existence and mutual well-being.

"As you do unto others, so it will be done unto you." If people exploit, they will be exploited by others and will reap turmoil. If a person synergizes by working with and for their neighbor, they will be given to; and peace will reign in their life.

I have not yet met a person who is not searching for this peace. I, too, am searching. I am searching for what can simply be called a better way of life. Humanity in general is tired of the violence, crime, and turmoil that flows through our society. You need not look far to find indications that we as a nation are all still searching for a better world ...a world of total love and peace.

If we do, indeed, seek to bring peace to the world, we can do it by first bringing peace to ourselves. A person cannot give that which they do not have. Until people find peace within themselves and can manifest it, they cannot teach others to be peaceful. They will be of no use to themselves or to others.

Balance is the key to synergism. As a person gains more awareness of their three levels of mind and learns to use those levels more productively, they will gain this necessary balance. When a human being has synergism, a mysterious third force enters their life...one plus one equals three not two. The whole becomes greater than the sum of its parts.

Humanity, as a whole, must learn to leave behind the "you or me" attitude of the past and begin to make the "you and me" or "you and us" attitude a total reality today! Living synergistically is a working "you and me" attitude.

ᏢEACE OF ᏫIND

Very little is needed to make a happy
life. It is all within yourself, in your
way of thinking."
             - Marcus Aurelius

I believe that the concepts discussed in this book, which form the basis of synergistic living, can bring you peace of mind. What is peace of mind? It is well-being. It is happiness. It is achieved when the four natures of a human being - health, wealth, love, and perfect self-expression - are in balance.

To help you visualize this, draw a square; and on one side write the word "Health." Many doctors are reporting today that 80% of all illness is psychosomatic. If this is true, then we must take a closer look at ourselves and the illnesses that we have, whether they be occasional or frequent. Could it be that illness is a manifestation of improper thinking? Could it be that illness is a manifestation of inner turmoil, confusion, doubt, worry, or fear? If any of these be true, then all that is necessary to alter our health is that we have a better understanding of ourselves - who we are, what we are, our purpose in life - and that we change our negative thinking.

It has been reported that people could live to be 140 or 150 years of age; but, instead, most people live to only about half that age. How is it possible to obtain perfect health if one now has illness? Without proper health, one cannot obtain perfect peace of mind.

A great many people go through life taking two aspirin tablets to solve their "headaches." They think that their problem is the headache, but in reality the headache is a result of some inner turmoil, confusion, or worry. It has been said that 84% of all worry is about things that will never come about; 12% of all worry is about things over which, at our present level of awareness, we have no control; 4% is legitimate worry. With these percentages, how does it pay to worry?

Worry is believed to be a major contributor to illness. Every day people crucify themselves between two thieves: one, the regret of lost opportunity; the other, the fear of what tomorrow may bring. Worry never accomplishes anything. When you have a problem, it is best to concentrate on the solution to that problem, not the problem itself. When the problem is overwhelming and there is not an apparent solution, forget it and move on to more productive thinking. This will give your subconscious a chance to work on the solution.

Now, on the opposite side of the square, write the word "Wealth." When speaking of wealth, we need not think in terms of millions of dollars. Many people have convinced themselves that the acquisition of masses of money and material things signifies the achievement of success and status. They think that they can gain respect by out-earning or out-buying those around them. But this is not true wealth. That is why many who seek happiness through material wealth are left wanting and dissatisfied. It is not money but what it can do that is important. Just having money or material possessions is not enough.

Wealth is a means to an end, not an end in itself. As a means, it can accomplish a great deal. Financial success is a worthy goal. Knowledge, achievement, and personal satisfaction are also indicators of wealth. What is important to understand when thinking of wealth is that money is not good or bad. Rather, a person's thoughts and actions determine the goodness or badness of their use of money. Wealth is a matter of "character." It is a state of mind. It is the result of proper thinking.

People are paid in direct proportion to the level of service that they render to humanity. If you desire to increase your income or wealth, simply increase your service. If you want to know of what service you are being to humanity, examine your wealth. To increase your service, find a need and fill it. The needs you fill might be in the area of ideas, products, or services. The more demand there is for your products, ideas, or services, the more you will be rewarded. It is the Law of Increase...you will be paid in direct proportion to the service you render to humanity. The end result is that you will have obtained liberty in the area of wealth.

On the top of the square, write the word "Love." when we refer to love, we are not speaking of the Greek 'eros" love, from which was derived the word erotic, or sexual love; nor are we speaking of "phileo" or brotherly love. We are speaking of "agapé" love, which is the "wishing or willing of good upon another."

Many people live in great turmoil because they are taught that they should "love thy neighbor" but cannot resolve how to love their neighbor when he or she does something they don't like or don't feel is right. To obtain peace of mind, one must love all people unconditionally. However, loving people does not necessarily mean that you must like what they do. One must learn to separate the person from the act. It has been said that a friend is "someone who knows everything about you and still loves you." This is unconditional love. You think good things about people instead of dwelling on their faults. You wish them well, instead of wishing them punishment or failure. You love them as opposed to judging them.

On the remaining side of your square, write the words "Perfect Self-Expression." Self-expression is a deep, innate urge to express and to fulfill potential talents and capabilities. It has to do with your emotional nature, or the emotional side of you. This side grows as you turn on the spigot and allow that universal power, that Godforce, to flow through you, expressing your perfect self. It increases as you learn to use your given talents more fully.

Through the conditioning of our society, we tend to learn suppressive techniques, rather than control techniques. Maturity within your emotional nature is controlling emotion: stopping negative emotions, and allowing positive feelings to flow.

Now that we have completed the peace of mind square, redraw it; but this time draw it in proportion to the way you feel about yourself. If your love is greater than your wealth, then make that side longer; and so on until you have measured each element. Then take a look at your square to see just how square it is....

Perhaps it will be helpful to relate this square to a chariot, with the four sides of your square representing four beautiful horses. If some of the horses are weaker and pull unevenly, the chariot will be thrown out of balance; and its journey will be disrupted. However, if all four horses – health, wealth, love, and perfect self-expression – pull together synergistically, the chariot will soar ahead to its destination.

Some people have interpreted the Book of Revelation as speaking of these natures when referring to the Four Horsemen of the Apocalypse. The pale horse is the physical or health side; the black horse represents the intellectual or wealth side; the red horse connotes emotions or the perfect self-expression side; and the white horse is the love or spiritual side. When a person understands these four sides or natures of their being and has them in balance, working synergistically, then they are in control of their destiny and can obtain perfect Peace of Mind.

The Search

*"Life demands that man must
confront situations -- sometimes to
change the situation, other times to
change himself..."*

Now that we are aware that the quest is inside each one of us; that it is a search for peace of mind; that it is an ability to feel good about ourselves physically, mentally, emotionally, and spiritually, we can begin to examine in detail exactly how to achieve this state of happiness.

A great many people foolishly believe that peace of mind will come to the degree that they are able to spend their time and money on luxuries for themselves. Some go to the extreme of taking their entire income and spending it on drinking, gambling, drugs, or so-called adult toys. They believe that having material things will make them happy. This belief has led some people to totally deny the responsibilities of their homes, depriving themselves and their families of the basic necessities of life. Some may even go to the extreme of leaving their responsibilities entirely in their quest for happiness. Sadly, these people have only made their search longer. Peace of mind becomes more distant with every action that takes balance out of their lives and adds to their inner turmoil.

Many people in today's society are very unhappy about themselves and their lives. They have no idea why they are living; they have no goals, no purpose other than day-to-day existence. The average person watches television between six and ten hours a day. These people go through life as inactive participants, living their lives through a fantasy, sitting in their living rooms. These people are so afraid to get out and make something of themselves that they play the game of escapism. Why? Perhaps it is because they have never accomplished anything of value and feel that they would be unable to accomplish anything, even if they should try. They have a program of defeatism. Their poor self-esteem results from a mind that has "bought" into negative programs of inadequacy.

Most people do not realize that they have had little control over their programming. It has been reported that 50% of our programming is absorbed by the time we are four years old, another 30% by the time we are eight. By the time we are in our twenties, we have "bought" programs like: "I'm just like my Dad..." or

"Everyone in my family has a temper ..." or "I'm a slow learner."

Become aware that most of our beliefs were learned unconsciously. We merely accepted or "bought" these programs. Because most people fail to realize this, they tend to make justifications for their failures by blaming life or circumstances. There are few people who have failed in life that do not have ample justification for their failures. Justification is a program too – one that has allowed them to accept their miserable lack of progress instead of rejecting it and doing something about it.

As we look back over our lives and see the mistakes that we have made, we cannot help but wonder if we will ever be able to change this pattern of failure into one of success. Unlike other creatures in this world whose programs are set and cannot be changed, a person can change their programs. Caterpillars will continue spinning their cocoons and birds will continue building their nests no matter what circumstances interfere, even if it means their own certain deaths, because these are their "programs." Human beings, however, can change their programs at will. All that is needed are the desire and the effort to do so.

Before growth can occur, we must have change. There is no growth without change. Imagine for a moment that you are in an airplane circling a distant city, and suddenly you must parachute out. You land in the wilderness. To reach your destination or to chart your route, you must first find out where you are. So it is with change. We must first become aware of where we are and recognize a need for change.

People's biggest problem in changing is in being totally aware and honest with themselves. As a person confronts the problems that have kept them from progressing in life, they become aware of the barriers they have created – barriers such as fear, insecurity, doubt, ill-health, poverty, hate, bigotry, prejudice, ego and greed. These barriers are manifestations of an ego problem. The ego problem is a result of a society that promotes exploitation. Being better than, prettier and smarter than, or richer than, at the expense of someone else, is an ego barrier. Only when a person confronts this problem, recognizes and admits where they are, will there be a possibility for constructive change. It is important to note here that when we speak of change, not all change is good. Change, as is true of all things, may be oriented towards growth or decay.

Constructive change comes when a person can look at themselves and feel happy about their achievements and even about their mistakes. "Show me a person who has made no mistakes, and I'll show you a person that has not yet lived." To understand our past mistakes and to neutralize the feelings of shame or guilt over our past inadequacies, we must understand that the acts we commit are neither good nor bad but are only wise or unwise depending upon our particular awareness at that time. We must learn to look at our mistakes, not as errors, but as growth opportunities. Our awareness increases as we learn from our mistakes.

When we look back at past situations with our newly acquired awareness, we may wonder how we could have been so naive or unintelligent. The real reason is, usually, that we were not as aware then as we are now. There is no possible way that we can be as aware at this moment as we will be in ten years. We must live and experience in order to grow in awareness. Mistakes contribute to an individual's learning and growth. "If I knew then what I know now" is a popular phrase, expressing this change. Accept that your life is, to date, the best that could be accomplished and that you will continue to improve as you grow in success and wisdom.

As an example, think of a young boy who has stolen a car. At that particular time in his life, perhaps he was unaware of the serious effects of his act. He knew that it was wrong; but with his lack of awareness, he was able to justify the wrong with, "It's only wrong if you're caught." Once a person understands that when they commit a crime, the crime is not against another person but against themselves, a major step in growth and awareness will have been taken.

"To thine own self be true" and "Love thy neighbor as thyself" are important concepts that must be digested before important growth can occur. With these concepts comes the desire for perfection of our feelings toward others; but if we hate ourselves, we cannot love another. "What you do not have you cannot give" is another way of saying it.

We all want to be all-loving and all-forgiving of others, yet we often are too harsh and demanding of ourselves. We must acquire balance between our feelings for ourselves and our feelings for others. We must learn first to be gentle with, appreciate, and like ourselves before we can appreciate and love other people. Wish yourself success, love, and faith first, and you will be surprised at how easy it will be to wish success on others.

To bring about a healthy self-image, a person must take control of their destiny and become a person who makes things happen. Generally speaking, people fall into two classes: the "think-offs," or those who know what is right and do nothing, and the "do-ers," or those who know what is right and do something about it. "Thought not committed to action is like a sun that never shines." Making things happen is what life is all about. Life is where all the action is. People will discover that when they start to work to make things happen, they will start to feel good about themselves and will experience greater peace of mind; they will develop balance and, with balance, they will gain liberty.

All people have freedom. Freedom is the right to make decisions. However, most people "will" this right to others (usually less competent than they are) because they are afraid to take responsibility for their decisions. What they fail to realize is that this, too, is a decision.

A person can make a decision in three ways: positively, negatively, or a decision not to make a decision. In all cases, a person is responsible for, and reaps the benefits or problems associated with that decision. To be successful, a person need only to make 51% of their decisions correctly. That means that you can be wrong occasionally and still live a very successful life. Since it is your life, doesn't it seem reasonable that you should be the one making the decisions with which you are going to live, instead of leaving such important matters to others or to chance?

Do not be afraid to make decisions. Decision-making is all important. The more decisions you make, the more accurate you will become. From the less wise decisions, you can learn and grow. As a result of making the right decisions, you will gain confidence and liberty – freedom to move in any direction at any time, at your will, when you decide. Few people gain liberty because few people choose to decide. Remember... "Not to decide is to decide."

Take control of your destiny. This is probably the greatest fear you will ever conquer. When you can confront yourself and take control of your life, then all other fears become incidental.

As in all things, there is a price to pay. The price is that you no longer can blame circumstances or luck for your situations. You and you alone must take responsibility for everything you do from now on. A person who has control over their own destiny does not recognize the words "luck" or "coincidence." This person understands that they make their own luck. They write their own story. They know what they want; they program it, and then they make it happen.

The Power
of the Mind

Mind is the Master Power that molds and makes
And Man is Mind, and evermore he takes
The Tool of thought, and shaping what he wills,
Brings forth a thousand joys, a thousand ills:
He thinks in secret and it comes to pass;
Environment is but his looking glass.
- James Allen

Everything which has ever been accomplished is a product of the Mind. Where is the Mind? The Mind is everywhere. What is the Mind? The Mind is everything. The Mind is the ultimate reality in the universe. Everything which we see and touch originated as a result of the creative power of the Mind. As was stated by Mahatma Gandhi, "Man is the center of a circle which has no circumference."

You are Mind. A person does not have a Mind. A person is Mind. Everything that a person is, including the conditions of success or failure which are a part of their life's experiences, are a result of Mind action.

Mind can best be understood in terms of three levels: the conscious, or self-awareness part of Mind; the creative, intuitive subconscious level; and the superconscious level, source of Universal Power. Mind is ONE, and these three levels are interrelated. They must function synergistically if their true potential is to be realized.

The conscious portion of the Mind has the responsibility for making decisions and exercising the power of choice. It has the ability to discriminate between what is desired and what is not desired. It is this part of Mind which sits in judgment. It determines what is wanted and is responsible for initiating action to get the desired results. The conscious mind knows persons, places, things, and conditions. The most important thing to remember about the conscious portion of the Mind is that it has the power of choice. It determines the direction in which the energies of the Mind are to be channeled.

The subconscious level of the Mind, on the other hand, is impersonal and acts only in keeping with its own nature…that of serving the conscious Mind. Its content, work, and expression are determined by the demands made upon it by the conscious Mind. It derives its strength from a higher level of Mind – the superconscious. Its storehouse is unlimited.

The subconscious receives, retains, and creates. It is the willing servant of the person who understands it and who uses their conscious Mind to intelligently direct it.

To control the functioning of the subconscious, however, the conscious Mind must first honestly believe that the wisdom and insight needed for the solution to a problem are available. This requires FAITH. The method, or "how," must be left to the subconscious Mind level.

Perhaps an analogy will help clarify this. Before a building is constructed, an architect must first plan out, in detail, everything which is going to be built. It all begins with an IDEA. Then a blueprint is created which describes the proposed structure – its location, size, weight, and materials from which it is to be built. Quite often, a model is made to help the architect visualize the "perfect end result." The architect BELIEVES that it can be built. All of this is done before the construction process actually begins.

This is true of everything that enters into and forms a part of our experience. Purposeful planning is the result of Mind activity. The conscious Mind may be thought of as the architect and the subconscious Mind as the construction engineer.

The architect (conscious Mind) goes over what he or she wants, in detail, with the construction engineer (subconscious Mind) before the building process is begun. Knowing that the engineer is an expert in his or her area, the architect trusts them to carry out the plans. The architect supplies the "what" and trusts the construction engineer to supply the "how." Without TRUST, the building would be a great idea never made real.

No building was ever built without proper materials. The construction engineer is responsible for getting the needed supplies. It is the superconscious which supplies the subconscious (construction engineer) with whatever materials are necessary to get the job done. The superconscious level of the Mind is the source of all things – perfect, true, and beautiful. One must remember that it is the architect (conscious Mind) who must first do the asking before the building can be built. It is the architect who determines the ultimate quality and size of the building. The materials are available from the source, or superconscious Mind, only when they are requested through the subconscious and when combined with an IDEA from the conscious Mind.

Why be an architect of little ideas when GREAT IDEAS can be actualized merely for the asking? Truth, beauty, and perfection are available TODAY! The MIND is far greater than we have imagined and has powers seldom recognized and rarely used. When you understand the nature and function of its process, the Mind will make available to you whatever you desire or need for your growth and happiness. It is to the Mind that we turn for the answers to life's meaning and to find order within the universe.

> *"Ask and it shall be given unto you…*
> *Seek and ye shall find…*
> *Knock, and it shall be opened unto you."*

You Become What You Think About

"Sow a Thought and you reap an Act;
Sow an Act and you reap a Habit;
Sow a Habit and you reap a Character;
Sow a Character and you reap a Destiny."

- unknown

In the last chapter, we discussed the mind and the power of the subconscious. To channel this power and make it work for you, you must completely digest this concept: "You become what you think about." If you think negatively, the mind has nothing to work on but negative thoughts. When you project problems, ill health, poverty or the like, the mind works overtime to create these things.

Accept for a moment that the mind is your "Genie." It will do exactly what you tell it to do. Now, recall some of the directions you have been giving Genie, such as: "I'm coming down with a cold...", "I won't be able to pay these bills this month", "I just can't stop smoking", "I'm pretty ignorant." Say these things out loud. How does it feel? What other things have you said today that are for your harm and not for your good? Strangely enough, most people, after some thought, are amazed at the negative programs that they possess. All day long, most people program their Genies for their destruction.

After looking over my personal life and after speaking with others concerning this point, of one thing I am sure: People get what they want in life when they reach the point at which they can see themselves having what they seek.

When I was a young boy, I wanted a bicycle so intensely that I just couldn't think about anything else. As I came from a poor family, the bike was almost out of the question at that particular time. But I dreamed and dreamed... saw myself riding the bike, washing it, fixing it. I went to work, saved, and bought that bike. Perhaps this example is elementary, but look back over your own life. You will find that those things which you wanted adamantly enough to see yourself having, and for which you were willing to pay the price, you received. It is important to note that merely dreaming is not enough. There is always a price to be paid.

Everything you are, and everything you have, started as a thought in your mind. Your body is merely there to manifest physically that which the mind tells it to do. Everything starts with you telling the mind what you desire.

Take hold of that Genie within, and start to program it for your good and for the good of humanity. Begin to get excited about YOU. Do not waste precious time on your faults. Change those faults by seeing them disappear. See the positive images instead. Only think about the fault once; then cross it out and see the image of the "new" YOU. Every minute, every hour, visualize the way you want to be. Get excited about that new YOU.

The foundation for the new YOU will be based on your values. Every person has values...they stand for something...they also need integrity. Integrity is defined by Webster as "adherence to a code of values." Sometimes, in order to have complete integrity, you will stand alone. You may at times lose friends, but you will find inner peace by staying with that in which you believe.

Too many people sell out their integrity for the want of being liked by all. If a person has the respect of their peers, they have something far more important. We all have been tested at one time or another; it is difficult to stand on "your rock" against the world. While it is more important to be respected than "liked," these two states do not necessarily oppose each other. More often than not, we tend to feel good about those people whom we also respect. We do not need to agree with a person to respect and like them. Indeed, that is what makes life and friendship interesting.

How, then, does one gain respect? To gain respect, begin by respecting yourself. Live up to your word. Do not, under any circumstances, go against that in which you believe. Do not exploit others. And, most importantly, start to love, wishing good and success to everyone you meet. When you start to respect yourself – when you know that you are strong enough that you would never violate your own principles – then you will begin to love yourself, like yourself, and be proud of yourself. A person that is happy with themselves is a person that others feel good to be around. When you love and respect yourself, you will find it easier to love and respect those around you.

Values and principles are learned and developed from early childhood. We, therefore, want to instill in our children a set of values that will carry them through life. A strong set of values will bolster a child against anything that tries to pull them down. Perhaps people today would not be so concerned with drugs, crime, and "identity" problems if they had been taught love and respect for themselves and had developed strong values as children.

"Think success and it will happen....
Think failure and it will happen..."

A person's future is formed by the thoughts they hold most often in their mind. Every person, at birth, is given an empty book. They are entitled to write their own story.

Begin today to write your own life story...your destiny. Start by writing down what you want out of life – where you will be in 10 years, 15 years, 20 years. What do you want for your family? This approach to writing down a life plan...mapping out your destiny...may seem awkward initially, but it is vital to goal achievement. So many people today seem to be "searching for their identity" – who they are, why they are here, what they should do, where they should go. If you are looking for yourself, believe me, you will never find "you" because you are what you believe you can become. You, and you alone CREATE your own identity. You have the right to become anything that you want: Wealthy? Yes! There are more millionaires being created today than ever before in the world. There are more advantages than ever before in all areas. Business, education, and government are crying out for leaders, people with ideas who want to make something of themselves and who are willing to earn that which they desire.

It has always seemed strange to me that most people will give more thought to buying a new car than to their life's work. So many people enter their life's vocation, not by choice, but by chance. Then they remain there, locked in, dissatisfied, waiting for the time that they can retire.

Stop looking at life through a keyhole...open the door to opportunity...get involved, and CREATE the YOU that you CHOOSE to become.

> *"Whatsoever things are true,*
> *whatsoever things are honest,*
> *whatsoever things are lovely,*
> *whatsoever things are of good*
> *report...think on these things."*
> *- Philippians 4:8*

Givers Gain, Takers Lose!

"The hand that gives – gathers"

You and you alone are totally responsible for your life. You and you alone are totally responsible for your peace of mind. If you do not have this peace of mind, you are not following the universal laws of God and humanity. One of the most important of these laws is that of "Givers gain and takers lose."

The law or concept that we are talking about in this chapter is one that you probably have heard before in many ways. If you do not have peace in your life, you, like many others, have probably not fully understood its message. You receive exactly what you put out, or, "As you sow, so shall you reap."

All the money in the world will not give you peace. No other person can give you peace. No one can solve your problems but you. Running to teachers and "gurus" for answers will not give you peace. Moving to a different location will not give you the peace you seek. None of these will give you peace because peace does not come from outside sources; it is obtained by going within and by following universal laws. The answers that you seek are already a part of you. You have only to understand and practice them. Only then will you become peaceful within yourself and with all humanity.

"A person is paid in direct proportion to the service that they render to humanity" is another way of saying, "As you sow, so shall you reap." If you give peace and love to everyone you know and meet, you will receive peace and love in return. If you are hateful and cruel, hatred and cruelty will enter your life.

We have been talking about several laws in these chapters, but this is by far the greatest law that has ever been written. Everyone has heard it. The simplicity of this law is perhaps the reason it is overlooked so often and not taken seriously. Obtaining peace is as simple as this: give peace and you will receive peace.

If you digest this law of becoming a giver and make it a part of your everyday life, you will receive such rewards that you will be astounded. But you must live it every moment of every day. You must turn the other cheek against all adversity, all misfortune. You MUST give love and wish success to everyone you meet.

People start early in life with the attitude of "getting the other fellow back." This is an immature attitude but one that many do not outgrow. When a child becomes angry at another child for breaking a toy, they have not yet learned to be tolerant and understanding. The child's first reaction is to hit back or to break the other child's toy. In children, this is excused and then explained.

As we grow into adulthood, however, "fully developed and mature," we need to learn to be tolerant of the mistakes of others and to give them space for growth. Let us understand that a fight does not begin until the second person strikes back. We teach by example.

Many people have given up trying to live "right" as a result of a misunderstanding of this one concept: "as you sow, so shall you reap." They have taken this concept to mean that whatever they put out comes back, (which is a correct assumption). However, they expect the returns to come back from the same source (which is not a correct assumption). That is just not the way the law works. This law guarantees that you will get exactly what you put out, but it does not say that it will come back from the same source. It only states that you will receive amounts of love and peace equal to what you have given.

Webster defines "giving" as "to make a present of." How often does a person truly give without the thought of something in return? When you give love, you expect love in return. When you give understanding to someone, you expect them to be understanding in return. When you give a gift, you usually expect a gift back, or you expect that the person will like you or respect you more for having given a gift. Few give just to give.

With this "I will if you will" attitude, disillusionment with the concept is likely to occur. When a person does not receive exactly or, perhaps, even more than that which was given, the tendency is to become hurt or even hostile and angry toward others. What we fail to realize is that all people have choices. They are individuals, just as we are. Because different people are motivated by different things, they may not respond in exactly the way we might want them to respond. It takes little effort to love and give to those who are giving and love us in return, but this is not what the law teaches. Feelings of resentment turn into revenge and cause inner turmoil, illness, and misery. When a person wishes ill for another, they are issuing the order for destruction to come into their own life.

*"Complete and absolute love is
within each and every one of us.*

To obtain this peace of mind, first let love come into your life – love for all. Scrutinize your mind and heart for all the feelings of resentment and hate toward others. Neutralize every bitterness you have toward anyone for whom you have had these feelings, and put in their place feelings of warmth and love and a wishing for their success. This may not be easy, but it can be done. You can find good in everything if you will only look. Find this good and begin to feel good about that person again. Dispose of all the anger in your life, and replace it with warmth and love. You need to do this before you can begin to feel good about yourself, before the love that is within you will begin to flow freely to everyone and to yourself.

When we can neutralize our negative feelings and become one with ourselves, then we can begin to reap the many rewards of peace in our lives. But then the battle has just begun. To remain a giver requires strength and a wholehearted commitment to these concepts. Many of the givers in life so often become intimidated by the takers because the takers are louder and so often appear stronger. Takers justify their actions with "all people do" and to make this come true, they forcefully try to persuade everyone they meet to become a taker with them. Only the truly committed givers will be able to survive.

The rewards in life are not measured by how much a person can gain by cheating on their income taxes, or by how much they can hurt others. The rewards come from how much can be given to assist others.

What service can you be to humanity? How much love can you give? How good a friend can you be? The rewards you will gain by becoming a GIVER will reap for you true peace and a feeling of beautiful wholeness.

When you stop worrying about what the other person thinks of you and start being concerned about what you think of yourself, things will begin to happen.

Begin now to neutralize your past negative feelings. Start to do things for the right reasons. When you become a person that you can love and respect, then you will be loved and respected by others. This is what you must strive for every day. Become a leader of GOOD, and help others by having the strength to overcome the hatred of the world.

When you start living your life as a giver, you

will fall in love with yourself, life, and everyone you meet.

TODAY IS THE FIRST DAY OF THE REST OF YOUR LIFE

This is the beginning of a new day. God has given me this day to use as I will. I can waste it – or use it for good, but what I do today is important, because I am exchanging a day of my life for it! When tomorrow comes, this day will be gone forever, leaving in its place something that I have traded for it. I want it to be gain, and not loss; good, and not evil; success, and not failure; in order that I shall not regret the price that I have paid for it.

- Dr. Heartsill Wilson

People can become anything that they want to become. Everyone has the ability – all that is needed is the will, a plan, and the power to put that plan into action. That is what I call the W.P.P. FACTOR: the WILL to put into action a POWERFUL PLAN.

Success is easier to obtain than failure. Everything in this universe is geared to success, not failure. When a person fails, they buck many odds. People do this by seeing failure, and the mind must then work overtime to achieve the end. The mind is a success-oriented mechanism. It works to keep us emotionally, spiritually, and physically in tune and in balance. When a person anticipates failure, the mind then goes against all that it knows in order to achieve that end result.

> *"Whatever the mind of a person can conceive and believe - IT CAN ACHIEVE."*

You must bring this concept into your life, digest it completely, and make it a part of you. Become aware of the "I AM" concept...what it is and from where it comes. It is the foundation upon which everything else rests. The "I AM" concept is infinite. It becomes finite only when people take hold of it and imposes their limitations.

When most are asked to quote their "I AM's," usually they come up with such things as: I am a father, a male, an engineer, six-foot one, 160 pounds; or, a mother, wife, secretary, and so on. They have limited themselves to exactly what they are. Where are the men and women of today who will shout: I AM GREAT... I AM A

LEADER? Where are the leaders of today? What has become of them? Why is this world made up of so many followers?

When I speak of becoming a leader, I am not speaking of leading a nation or even a corporation, although those are, indeed, worthy goals. Rather, I am speaking of becoming a leader of yourself... becoming a leader of your own destiny, taking control of yourself and your life, becoming a leader of your home, a leader among your friends, and especially a leader of your children.

The only limitations upon you are those which are self-imposed. People must confront themselves and say, "I am a leader..." "I am strong, healthy, and a genius..." "I am a leader with a strong set of values that I always live up to..." "I have integrity..." "I am working at becoming in tune with myself and the world around me..." "I am working at controlling my destiny ..." "I decide my fate; I create my luck. I have taken control."

"You save your life by spending it."

You have the ability to start today to become a leader. It makes no difference whether you are 18 or 80, male or female. Your maker has endowed you with every tool necessary to learn and to become successful, and he/she expects you to use these tools for the betterment of humanity.

Just because you are seventy is no excuse to give up and let others make your decisions for you. The fact that you are still alive is reason enough to believe that you are here for a purpose; and that purpose is to learn, to teach, and to GIVE.

Take control now. Forget about the negative thoughts which others have told you – that you are too old or too young. Stop letting the thoughts of others rule your life; stop being weak and cowardly, blaming your lack of progress on those negative programs. If you begin now and become a do-er, you will have earned your right to remain here. Let your life mean something. Become an inspiration to others so that they may try to do more and to become more than they are today.

In a recent study of longevity, 600 variables – such as nutrition, exercise, marital status, number of children, geographical location, lifestyle, etc. – were compared. The experimenters found that the variable which was most significant was "how varied and complete the life was." Contrary to what one might expect, those who lived comparatively easy lives seemed to die earlier than those who had suffered or who had complicated lives risking and living more dangerously.

"Be present at your own life."

Live dangerously; take risks; cultivate eccentricity, which means growing closer to being yourself. This will give you a life worth living and of which you can be proud.

Today is the first day, but it could also be the last day, of your life. You have no guarantee that you will be here tomorrow. So live today as if it were your last day, and I know that you will live your life more fully. With so little time, there are just not enough minutes left to hate, not enough time for gossip or fighting. We should all be so busy "doing" and "being" that we have no time left for anything but accomplishing "good."

"Use it or you will lose it."

I would like to relate a story about living your life to the fullest. There once was a farmer who had three trusted employees a ranch foreman, a tractor driver, and a picker-upper. All had served faithfully throughout the years. One day the farmer called them into his office to talk with them about freedom and liberty – the freedom of doing what they wanted, when they wanted, and about what each wanted to do with their lives. The farmer told them that he wanted them to have freedom and liberty.

To the ranch foreman he said, "You've been with me for twenty years, and I want to see that you have the opportunity to experience liberty so I am giving you $200,000. Go out and buy your own business; do your own thing. Come back in one year, and bring me a small percentage of the profit you make."

To the tractor driver, he said, "You have had less responsibility and have been with me fewer years, but you have been faithful; and I want to reward you. Here is $100,000. Do what you want to do, but bring me a percentage of your profit in one year."

To the picker-upper, he said, "You have been with me only a few years and have held fewer responsibilities, but you, too, deserve an opportunity to get ahead. Here is $50,000. Go, and return in a year."

As was agreed, a year later the three men came back to settle their accounts. The picker-upper was the first to respond. "Well, Sir, I was thinking about all that money. It's been a bad year for business, and $50,000 is a lot of money – more than I've ever seen at one time. The government isn't too stable right now; prices keep going up, and the value of the dollar keeps going down, and the banks might fail...I was so afraid that I would lose your money that I protected it by burying the $50,000 in a tin can...and see, here it is – all of it – I brought it back"

The tractor driver then replied, "Well, I'll tell you, Boss, things were bad out there, so I took some of the money and put it in the bank and got a few percent interest on it. Then I put the rest in blue chip stocks and made a little profit. Here is the $100,000 plus the interest."

The ranch foreman then answered, "Well, Sir, it's been some year...I went out and bought some cattle, and they caught a disease and died on me. But I salvaged some of the money, and I went into farming and some other things. I got into a small business, and I really lost pretty heavily at first; but I worked hard and very long hours...and by the end of the year things worked out pretty well. So here's your $200,000 back and $100,000 more."

The farmer then took the $50,000 from the picker-upper and gave it to the ranch foreman...

". . . and he that had not, even that
which he had was taken from him
and given to him that had . . ."

This story, of course, is taken from the Bible story of the Talents. It means this: If you have something and you don't use it, you will lose it. It is called the Universal Law of Use. You must use your given talents, or you will lose them.

If you live just for today, to make today the most successful, happy day of your life, I am sure that you will have an extraordinary life. A successful life is nothing more than a series of successful days. It is easy to take life one day at a time. Try to make the most of life; live by the concepts: love everyone you meet, and wish yourself love and success.

It also helps if you have a goal. If you keep your eye on that goal, all things will work towards attaining it. Also, cultivate friends with whom you share some of the same goals. Jesus surrounded himself with do-ers that had the same end in sight as he. That is one of the many reasons he was able to keep to his goal.

Start today to become a searcher of good – of love and of world peace. Start to use your three levels of consciousness. Allow this universal power to flow freely through you. Become its vehicle in bringing about peace to humanity. By bringing balance into our lives and into the lives of everyone that we touch, we can all pull together for one end – World Peace. Accept completely a YOU and ME attitude. Start to live it, and you will begin to live your life more abundantly. You will have begun to truly "Live Synergistically."

The morn of a new day
is just dawning
The freedom of the
day awaits you –
You Are...
We Are...
Together.

- Thomas Dale Willhite

PSI Seminars is a leading provider of educational seminars. Founded in 1973, PSI Seminars presents a variety of seminars on leadership, communication and vision. These comprehensive educational programs provide tools for gaining freedom, control, abundance, professional success and happiness in life.

If you have enjoyed and found useful the concepts and ideas expressed in this book and would like to become more fully involved in developing your potential and living life synergistically, we invite you to correspond with us concerning any of the following:

1. Additional copies of LIVING SYNERGISTICALLY are available for $12.95 ea.

2. Information concerning our seminars.

3. Information concerning other PSI products.

We encourage you to find us on the world wide web at:

http://www.psiseminars.com

or feel free to write us via email at:

psipublishing@psiseminars.com

or via traditional mail at:

PSI PUBLISHING
11650 High Valley Road
Clearlake Oaks, CA 95423
707.998.2222

Notes

Notes

Notes

Notes

Congratulations for choosing to read "Living Synergistically." We would like to extend to you an invitation to continue using PSI's personal development products by sending you one complimentary audio product of our choosing.

All you have to do is remove and fill out the back side of this card completely, pay the price of one stamp, drop it in the mail and we will send you out your complimentary audio product.

PSI Seminars

Name _____

Address 1 _____

Address 2 _____

City _____

State _____

Zip _____

Country _____

Phone _____

Fax _____

E-mail _____